Jesse Hartley

DOCK ENGINEER TO THE PORT OF LIVERPOOL 1824–60

NANCY RITCHIE-NOAKES

MERSEYSIDE COUNTY MUSEUMS

© COPYRIGHT 1980
ISBN 0 906367 05 0
SET IN 'MONOPHOTO' EHRHARDT BY AUGUST FILMSETTING, STOCKPORT, CHESHIRE
PRINTED BY ROCKLIFF BROTHERS LTD, LONG LANE, LIVERPOOL
DESIGNED BY BARRIE JONES

Contents

Jesse Hartley 1780–1860

Who was Jesse Hartley?

Who was Jesse Hartley?

When Isambard Kingdom Brunel's famous iron ship *Great Britain* was launched in Bristol by Prince Albert on the 19th July, 1843, she was larger than any vessel then in existence – and the dock entrance was not deep enough for her to pass through. But she found a suitable berth in Liverpool, and from there she operated a service to New York. The man who planned and built the docks that could accommodate what was then the largest ship in the world was Jesse Hartley.

Jesse Hartley was born in Pontefract, Yorkshire on 21st December, 1780. His father was a stonemason, architect and bridgemaster and Jesse's earliest professional works were executed in the West Riding under his father's direction. Until his appointment in 1824 as Civil Engineer and Superintendent of the Concerns of the Dock Estate in Liverpool, Hartley concentrated on the design and construction of masonry bridges. By then his experience of bridgebuilding was very wide – it ranged over works in Yorkshire, Lancashire, London and Ireland. His appointment to the important Liverpool job is interesting because he had no direct experience of dock construction, and among the thirteen rival applicants were several well-known engineers. Nevertheless, Hartley's appointment as dock surveyor gave him the chance to express the grandiose ideas and expend the prodigious energies which became the trademarks of his tenure.

Jesse Hartley's works in Liverpool were extensive: in the 36 years from 1824 to 1860, during which he served the Dock Trustees, he constructed or altered every dock in the city; he added no less than 140 acres of wet docks and some 10 miles of quay space; he was consultant engineer to the Liverpool and Manchester Railway Company; he was involved in construction of the high level coal railway and the Liverpool end of the Leeds and Liverpool Canal. Jesse Hartley is said to have been devoted to his work, and the quantity and quality of his projects indicate that his life must have been little more than his work. Thus keys to an assessment of Hartley lie in his works – those monuments and records of the man, variously called artist and despot, who styled himself engineer, architect and surveyor.

Hartley the dock engineer

Early in November, 1824, less than eight months after his appointment, 'Mr. Hartley, the Dock Surveyor, . . . laid before the Trustees of the Docks a General Plan of Dock Works for the Improvement and Accommodation of the Port, accompanied by a very full report thereon.'[1] He had not wasted any time. His plans for dock works included construction of a river wall and works to the north of Princes Basin as well as schemes for the Dry Dock, the Salthouse Dock, the Brunswick Basin, the proposed Brunswick Dock, the South Basin and the Graving Dock. The Dock Bill which had been formulated mainly on the basis of the Surveyor's recommendations received the Royal Assent on the 27th June, 1825. Similar enabling acts, to allow the Dock Trust to raise revenue and govern its estate, were an integral part of the management of that estate, and the pattern of plan preparation, submission, argument, production of expert witnesses and so on became a familiar one to Mr Hartley. The Liverpool docks built under his direction were Clarence, Brunswick, Waterloo, Victoria, Trafalgar, Albert, Canning Half-tide, Salisbury, Collingwood, Stanley, Nelson, Bramley-Moore, Wellington, Wellington Half-tide, Huskisson and Canada Docks.

Hartley's plans for new docks were hardly revolutionary, but he was responsible for several important innovations and his position gave him a unique opportunity to deal with each of his docks as a part of a whole system. Despite his predilection for curious architectural styles, he was a pragmatist. When planning what has become his most famous monument, the Albert Dock warehouses, he not only made models of the brick arches which he proposed for the new buildings but also conducted an experiment to ascertain '. . . how long sheet iron placed as a ceiling, under a wooden floor, could resist fire'.[2] For the purposes of the latter he constructed a building 18 feet square and 10 feet high in the Dock Yard and invited Dock Committee members to watch him set fire to it. The timber resisted combustion for 40 minutes. One of the results of the experiment was a design for an iron framed incombustible warehouse.

Hartley evidently made a systematic effort to inform himself of both general scientific developments and specialist advances in his own professional fields. His will lists plans, models (mathematical and philosophical), a microscope and other instruments as among the treasured possessions left to his son. He was eager to use new structural materials in his works and was interested in new patents and inventions. The Albert Dock warehouses exhibit some novel uses of iron, and they were equipped with hydraulic cargo-handling and dock machinery. Hartley's business trips were sometimes to seek and sometimes to give counsel on architectural and engineering matters. Such contact, often with other eminent engineers such as James Walker, George Stephenson and George Aitchison, must have been stimulating and useful to Jesse Hartley. For instance, enclosed dock-warehouse systems were pioneered in London in the early nineteenth century. The new docks offered two distinct advantages: with the use of locks to impound the water at a constant level, loading and unloading were unaffected by the rise and fall of the tides; and the docks were enclosed by high boundary walls which reduced opportunities for pilfering. The St Katharine's development in London was the first in which the warehouse blocks were built hard up against the water's edge so that cargoes could be hoisted directly from ships' holds into warehouses. Hartley improved on this cargo-handling system by incorporating crane arches in his design for the Albert warehouses. In 1843 Hartley wrote to Philip Hardwick, architect of the St Katharine's Dock warehouses, confessing himself to be somewhat new to the business of designing large scale warehouses and asking Hardwick's opinion of his (Hartley's) proposed scheme for the Albert Dock. One result of this consultation was Hardwick's collaboration with the project, though Hartley's was, of course, the last word on disputed matters.

Hartley's meticulous attention to every detail of each project under his superintendence is shown first in the design and then as completely in its execution. He liked things done properly. The S. & J. Holme's contract for bricks for the Albert Dock specified bricks '... manufactured of the Clay called the North Shore Clay ... to be hard burned and well shaped ... and without any admixture of Clinkers or of broken or of Soft Bricks or Bricks containing Lime pebbles ... And it is hereby agreed that the Surveyor of the said Docks shall have the sole and uncontrolled power ... of rejecting all such of the said Bricks as he may in his own judgment deem soft, badly shaped or in the slightest degree defective ... or otherwise unsatisfactory to the Surveyor of the said Docks in any manner howsoever.' Further, the rejected bricks had to be removed from the building site–within 24 hours, at Holme's expense. Only the value of the contract and, presumably, Holme's confidence in their product can have compensated for the many penalty clauses imposed on them by the Surveyor.

Hartley the entrepreneur

Not infrequently did questions about the management of the Surveyor's Department arise. Judging by the number of rows recorded in the Minutes of the Dock Committee and by remarks about his associates contained in Hartley's personal correspondence, he was not always an amenable individual. Such a personality vested of relatively great power and influence was bound to arouse antagonism, and assaults on Hartley's reputation were not uncommon. Of course, the Dock Trustees were rightly concerned about the effectiveness of their expenditure of hundreds of thousands of pounds every year. An 1836 report on the Dock Surveyor's Department reveals an extensive and impressive direct labour force. Seventeen blacksmiths and twenty assistants were employed in the blacksmith's forge and shop, where all the forged iron work required about the docks for gates, bridges, etc was prepared, and all machinery fitted up. There were also millwrights', carpenters', and shipwrights' workshops, a brass foundry and a painter and plumbers' shop. Masons, sawyers and paviours with their assistants and a number of labourers made up the full Dock Yard complement. The office staff comprised Mr Hartley, Mr Gilbert Cummins, who was the principal clerk, and Mr Thomas Packinson, the storekeeper, who was 78 years old in 1836 and said to be retained 'more on account of his length of service than his present efficiency'[3]. By 1841, the number of persons of the various trades employed under the Dock Surveyor was 528. The outcome of an investigation into the management of the Dock Yard in that year was nevertheless extremely favourable in its findings: 'The Sub-Committee . . . are unanimously of opinion . . . that the various works have been executed on very reasonable terms, and at lower rates than they could have been in any other way . . .'[4].

Hartley's comprehensive control of his operations extended beyond the supply and management of labour to the supply and management of materials. He was not a man who could tolerate waste of time or money. He once reported to the Dock Committee that he had on hand some small paving stones, unfit for pavement of the quays, which he proposed to break up for rubble for a cart road.[5] After requesting permission to order some cast iron stanchions, he found that he had some oak which would be equally suitable and returned to the Committee to ask for approval to use the material on hand.[6] He also reported that he had sold some old doors and other materials for £12.6.7. and an old pump for £12.12.0.[7] Reporting on the re-building of George's Dock, he wrote, '. . . this work was regularly advertised, and let by Contract to the lowest offer . . . The Contractor afterwards became dissatisfied with his Contract.[This was a recurring hazard.] For the sake of despatch I took from him the objectionable part of his Contract, which I had performed under my own direction; and in that portion, I saved the Dock Estate £1,448.12s 11½d., which would have been paid to the Contractor, had he fulfilled the whole of his Contract.'[8] Hartley's most ambitious cost-cutting scheme involved opening a granite quarry at Kirkmabreck, Kirkcudbright-shire, and commissioning a coaster called *Oak* for the purpose of carrying large blocks of granite and timber. Five years after the quarry was opened, and including the costs thus incurred, Hartley reckoned to be saving 8½d. per foot on ashlar and 6¾d. per ton on setts. As he wrote off the capital investment (*Oak* cost £2,186.6.8., although estimated only at £1,800) over the years, the price of fine stone for the dock works would continue to fall.

Hartley's mental and physical energies must have been prodigious. His numerous responsibilities as Dock Surveyor are cited in his annual reports to the Dock Committee. The report for the year ending 24 June, 1850 lists the following projects, all precisely costed, which had occupied the Surveyor and his department during the preceding year: new works on some ten docks, the dock railway, warehouses, the landing stage, police huts, telegraph stations and conversion of the old lightship *North Star* into a schooner for carrying granite; general repairs including dredging and scuttling away mud, towing mud boats, paving and lighting quays, repairing bridges, gates, cloughs, landing waiters' huts, customs' depots, sheds, etc.; repairs and cleaning of graving docks and blocks; supplies and materials for steps and slips, police stations and houses, weighing machines, cranes, buoys, fire engines, life boats, telegraph buildings, marine parades, lighthouses, lightships and transit sheds. The Surveyor's total expenditure on these dock works in the financial year 1849–50 was £314,847.0.7., a typical annual sum.

Hartley the architect

Hartley the dock engineer was ever concerned to provide the longest runs of quay and the easiest and safest access for shipping. He was also aware of the importance of intercommunication within the docks, and between the docks and canals, railways and roads. Hartley the architect is less easy to analyse.

Before coming to Liverpool, Jesse Hartley worked for John Carr, a noted architect in the Palladian style. In Ireland Hartley worked for the Duke of Devonshire who also employed the architect William Atkinson; Atkinson specialised in Gothic and castellated styles. It has been suggested that Hartley's work shows also the influence of Thomas Harrison who designed the Chester Grosvenor Bridge which Hartley built to Harrison's specifications.[9] But much of Hartley's work is utterly distinctive and beyond pastiche. It is also breathtaking, sometimes amusing, always interesting and occasionally beautiful. Picton was particularly scathing about Mr Hartley's more outrageous structures, such as the (now demolished) hydraulic accumulator tower, at Canada Dock, which '. . . . is a lofty structure in grey granite with some subordinate attached buildings in a sort of castellated style. Whatever may have been the merits of Mr Jesse Hartley as an engineer–and they are undoubtedly great–a feeling for the beautiful was certainly not one of them. This tower is double, having a broad and a narrow side surmounted by an immense machiolated parapet . . . The upper part is decorated with spears, axes, and swords . . . with what meaning or intention it would be hard to say' (Sir J.A. Picton, *Memorials of Liverpool*, 1872). One can see Picton's point; Hartley's aesthetic forte was as a stone-mason. The beauty of his buildings lies in their fitness for their purpose and in their details worked in stone. The same may be said of his dock works where great attention has been paid not only to good detailed design, but also to the highest standards of composition and finish.

Hartley's Liverpool

Economic factors well beyond Mr Hartley's province gave him the opportunity and the means to realise his monumental visions. By the beginning of the nineteenth century Liverpool was the distribution port for the manufacturing districts of Lancashire, Yorkshire and the Midlands. International trade with the West Indies, the United States and West Africa continued to grow, and the breaking of the East India Company's monopolies opened the Indian and Chinese markets to Liverpool merchants. The capital accumulated as a result of increased trading activity was invested in infrastructure to handle more trade. The opening of the Liverpool and Manchester Railway in 1830 marked the beginning of railway transport and was the start of a vast railway network linking Birmingham (1837), London (1838), Birkenhead and Chester (1840) and Bury (1846). Related new capital works were the docks, quays, warehouses and other port facilities necessary for the increasing volume of goods to be handled. Jesse Hartley was quite equal to the challenge of dramatic increases in trade and shipping and he worked apace to provide Liverpool with the means to handle, store and despatch the ever greater tonnages the shipping companies and merchants directed through his port. Having spent nearly half his life working in Liverpool, Jesse Hartley died at home in Bootle on August 24th, 1860 and was buried under a plain granite headstone at St Mary's, Bootle. A road-widening scheme has displaced his gravestone, and reconstructions have obscured and obliterated some of his dock works, but many impressive memorials remain. On the following pages are some samples of the architectural and engineering legacies of Jesse Hartley.

Notes

1. Minutes of the Dock Committee, 29th January, 1824, Mersey Docks and Harbour Board Collection, Merseyside County Museums.

2. Minutes of the Dock Committee, 18th May, 1843, Mersey Docks and Harbour Board Collection, Merseyside County Museums.

3. Reports of Sub-committees of the Dock Committee, November, 1836, Mersey Docks and Harbour Board Collection, Merseyside County Museums.

4. Minutes of the Dock Committee, 21st May, 1841, Mersey Docks and Harbour Board Collection, Merseyside County Museums.

5. Minutes of the Dock Committee, 17th August, 1824, Mersey Docks and Harbour Board Collection, Merseyside County Museums.

6. Minutes of the Dock Committee, 2nd November, 1824, Mersey Docks and Harbour Board Collection, Merseyside County Museums.

7. Minutes of the Dock Committee, 17th May, 1825, Mersey Docks and Harbour Board Collection, Merseyside County Museums.

8. The Surveyor's Report to the Dock Committee on the General State and Progress of the Dock Works, October, 1836, Mersey Docks and Harbour Board Collection, Merseyside County Museums.

9. Robert Lamb, C.ENG, MI STRUCT E, Department of Architecture, Liverpool Polytechnic.

Acknowledgements

Michael Anthony Clarke, for consultancy on mechanical engineering, canal construction and railways.
Robert Lamb, C.ENG, MI STRUCT E, Department of Architecture, Liverpool Polytechnic for information from his original research into the engineering aspects of Hartley's work.
The Mersey Docks and Harbour Company for access to archive material.
Birmingham Public Libraries for access to the Boulton & Watt Collection.

Photographs

All photographs have been taken by Merseyside County Museums photographers Colin Pitcher and David Flower, with the exception of the following:
7. University of Liverpool Archives
13. City of Liverpool, Engineers Department
27, 30. Robert Lamb, Liverpool Polytechnic.

Plans and drawings

All plans and drawings are in the Merseyside County Museums Mersey Docks and Harbour Board Collection, with the exception of the following: 6, 15, 18, 24, 45 – Mersey Docks and Harbour Company.

MAWDSLEY'S MAP
OF THE
Town Port and Environs of
LIVERPOOL
BASED ON THE
Ordnance Survey
And specially revised and corrected to the present time
BY
PARK RYDER & WRENNALL Land Surveyors &c.
1871

Diagram showing the extent of Jesse Hartley's physical contribution to the growth of the town and docks of Liverpool during his period of office as dock engineer. The development of the dock system and the economy of the city were inextricably linked. But the magnitude of Hartley's contribution to Liverpool's prosperity cannot be measured in acres of docks alone: not only did he respond to the seaport's capacity for growth in his own day, but he laid the foundations for the trade which gave Liverpool a dominant position in the British economy right up until the First World War.

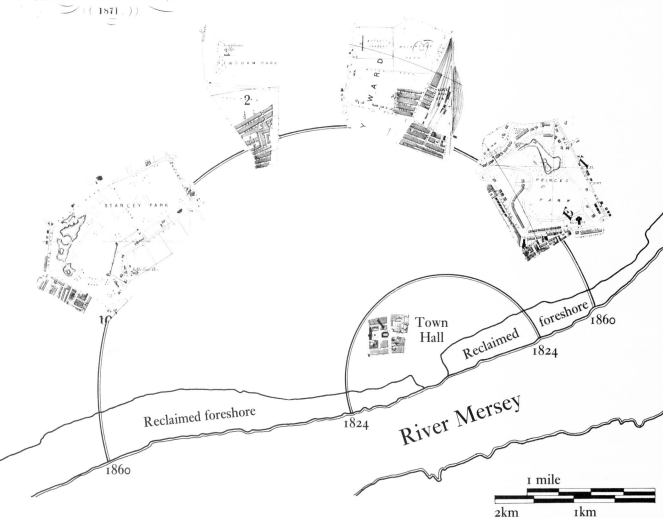

Map details from Mawdsley's Map of Liverpool not to scale.

1 Hartley's hydraulic accumulator tower at Canada Dock which caused Sir James Picton to write in his *Memorials of Liverpool* (1872), 'Whatever may have been the merits of Mr Jesse Hartley as an engineer–and they are undoubtedly great–a feeling for the beautiful was certainly not one of them.'

Hartley the architect

2 A characteristic pseudo-mediaeval edifice – the Dock Master's Office at Salisbury Dock, built in 1848. The 'cyclopean' (an ancient style of masonry in which the stones are immense and irregular in shape) construction is also typical.

3 The Victoria Tower, built by Hartley in 1848 at the entrance to
Salisbury Dock.
Jesse Hartley's designs can not be mistaken for the work of another.

4 Whether inspired by an architectonic whimsy or a philosophical preference, Hartley's castellated buildings are his architectural trademark. This is his 1834 design for Point Lynas lighthouse.

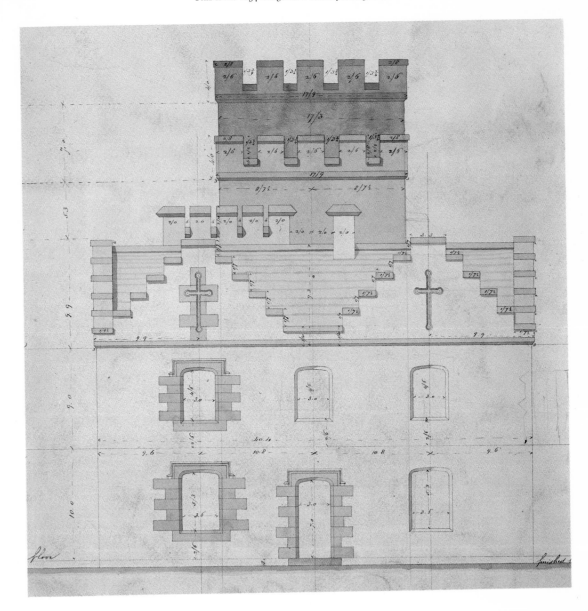

5a Elevation of a proposed lighthouse for Point Lynas by Robert Stevenson & Son, Edinburgh, 1834.

5b Elevation of a proposed lighthouse for Point Lynas by Jesse Hartley, Liverpool, 1834.

6 Philip Hardwick's design for the clock turret, Albert Dock warehouses. Clocks are important dockland features where access to basins and docks is restricted to but a few hours around the high tides.

7 The Hartley warehouse surmounted by Hardwick turret; the clock tower bears little affinity to the massive warehouse and looks as if it is a feature of another building altogether.

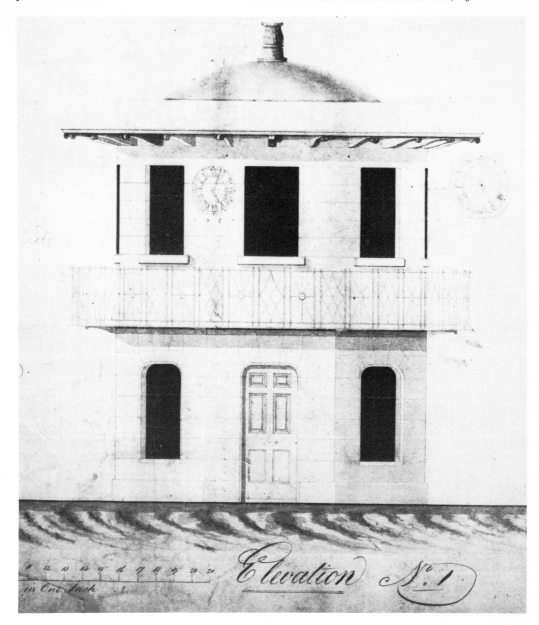

10 Hartley's 1834 elevation of the Dock Master's Office, Trafalgar.

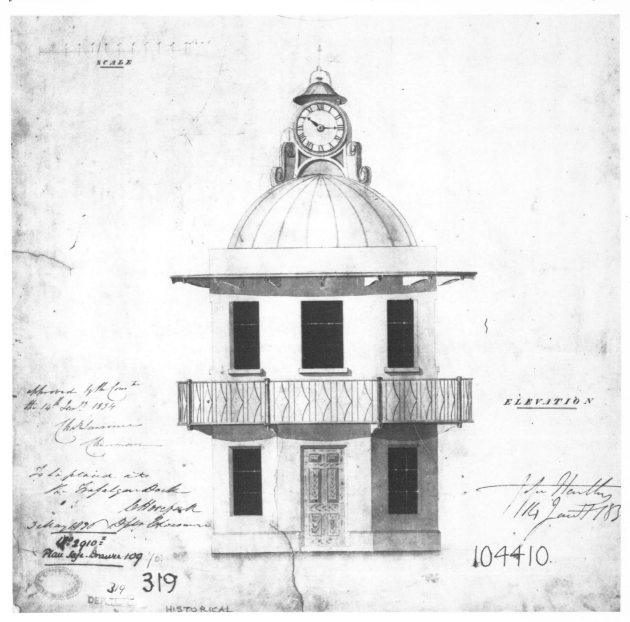

12 Gatemen's hut with stone roof, Canning Island, at the river entrance to the Canning Half-tide Basin.

13 Aerial view Albert Dock and warehouses, from the west. 'The Albert Dock and Warehouses, and the Canning Half-tide Dock, are founded partly on rock and partly on marl; but all the west and north sides of the Albert Dock, the south side of the Half-tide Basin, and the whole of the river wall in front thereof, and the piers in the double entrance from the river into the Half-tide Basin, are on quick sand, and have been built upon 13,792 piles of beech timber, the aggregate length of which would amount to over 48 miles. The quay walls of the dock are 40 feet deep below the coping. The warehouses are 66 feet in height above the coping, and cover a surface of 21,390 square yards, and are wholly constructed of stone, brick, and iron, and perfectly fire-proof, no timber whatsoever being used in them. The total cost of these works, complete, amounted to £514,475 8s 1d.'
(Baines's *History of the Commerce and Town of Liverpool*, 1852.)

Hartley's Albert Dock and Warehouses

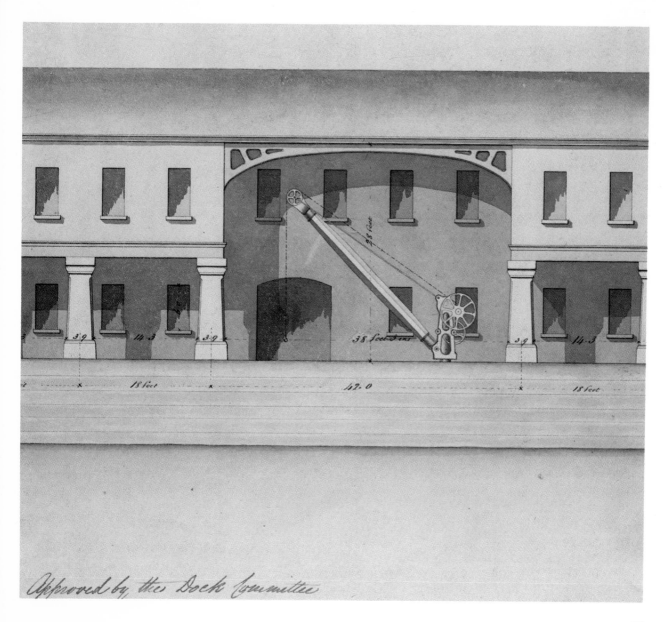

Approved by the Dock Committee

16 An early plan showing a layout for warehouses for a 'new dock'. The column spacing shows that consideration had not yet been given to the large crane arches which became an important feature of the Albert warehouses as built.

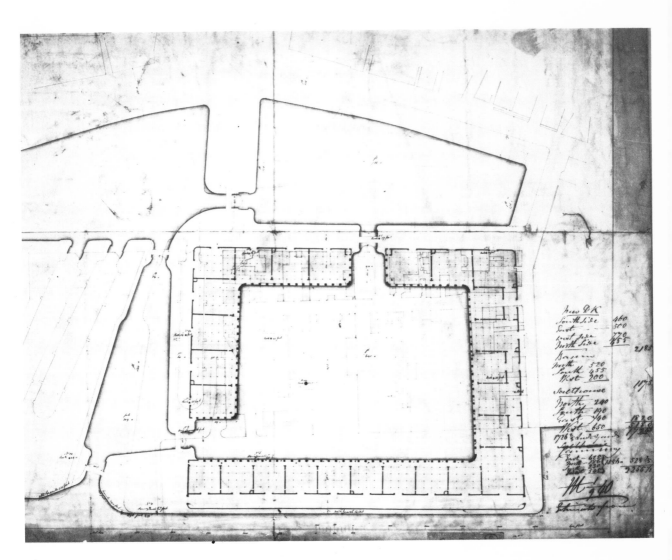

17 Another early warehouse scheme indicates the use of iron columns but does not relinquish timber floor joists and planks or timber roof trusses. Multi-storey iron frame mills had been built in England since the end of the eighteenth century, but the architects of dock warehouses were very slow to adopt this form of construction.

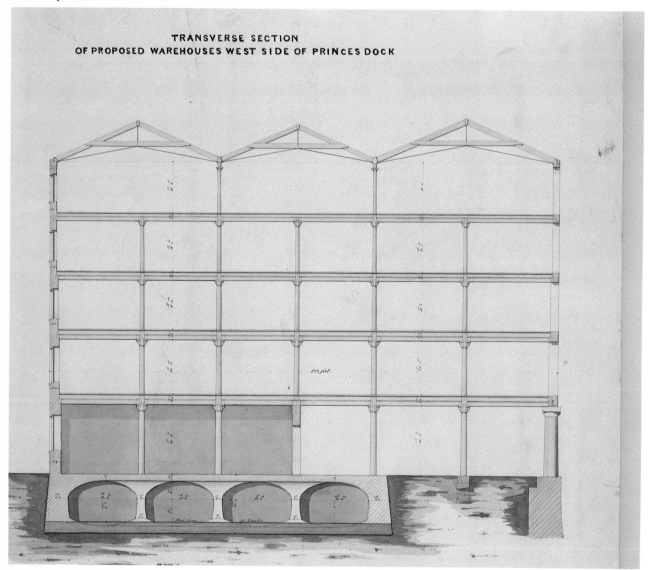

TRANSVERSE SECTION
OF PROPOSED WAREHOUSES WEST SIDE OF PRINCES DOCK

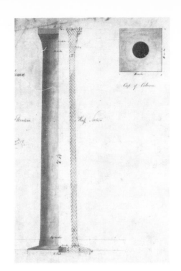
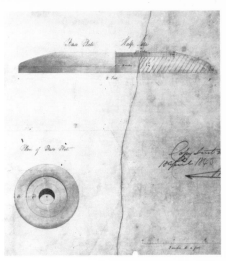

18a Elevation, section and plan of cast iron column for Albert warehouse vaults sent to the Haigh Foundry Co, near Wigan. Other well-known suppliers of cast iron work to the Liverpool docks included Wm Hazeldine, the Phoenix Foundry and Edward Bury.

18b Elevation, plan and section of cast iron beam for Albert warehouse vaults, sent to the Haigh Foundry Co in 1843. The contract for the Albert columns and beams was, in fact, awarded to J. & E. Walker of Gospel Oak Iron Works, another famous foundry.

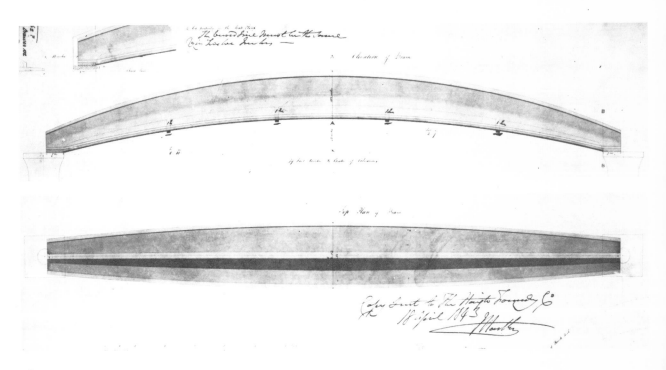

19 The vaults of the Albert Dock warehouses.
During the period 1830–50, cast iron was the most important material used by structural engineers. By then its strength and properties were known; it was useful in 'fire-proof' buildings, and the variety of forms in which it could be cast encouraged its use for ornamental purposes.

20a Detail of iron swing bridge across the northern entrance to Albert Dock. The parts for this bridge were cast at the Haigh Foundry.

20b Longitudinal section of one leaf of swing bridge for the 60 ft entrance, south end of Queen's Dock. John B. Hartley, 1855.

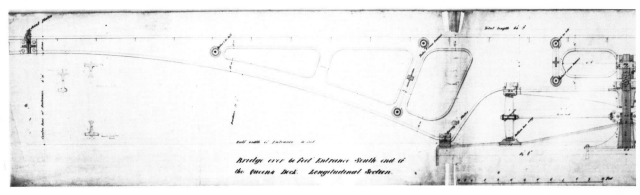

21 The view from Coburg (opened 1816) to Queen's Dock (opened 1796) in 1895, with iron swing bridge mounted in 'cyclopean' granite masonry. These two docks were constructed by John Foster and Thomas Morris respectively, but extensively altered by Jesse Hartley.

22a Elevation and sections of iron beams for the Albert Dock offices, sent to the Gospel Oak Iron Works.

22b Philip Hardwick's design for the front elevation of the Albert Dock offices.

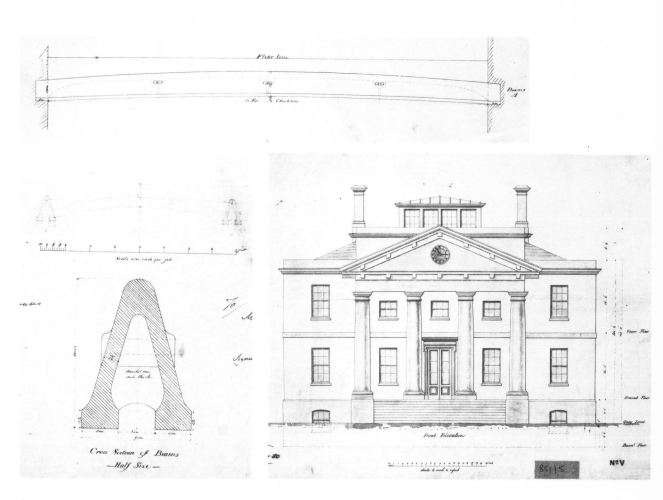

Cross Section of Beams
—Half Size—

Front Elevation

23 The Albert Dock offices as built. Hartley modified Hardwick's design by the addition of a top storey. The columns, entablature and pediment are cast iron.

24 Although smooth and corrugated wrought iron plates had been used before in roof construction, Hartley's use of wrought iron plates on the Albert warehouses is significant: his plates are riveted together to form one of the earliest examples of a curved, stressed skin construction. There are no purlins in the roof which is tied across the eaves by wrought iron bars supported by hangers from the tee section roof ribs. The galvanised iron plates are 10ft × 2ft 6in × $\frac{5}{8}$ in thick.

25 Cast iron quayside columns in the Albert Dock warehouses. The hollow columns have no base plates but are simply let into a chase in the 2 ft thick granite coping on the quay edge.

27 Plans of masonry courses, Clarence Graving Dock, 1831. Each stone is colour coded to show when and by which contractor it was laid. Monthly running totals of numbers of stones were also recorded.

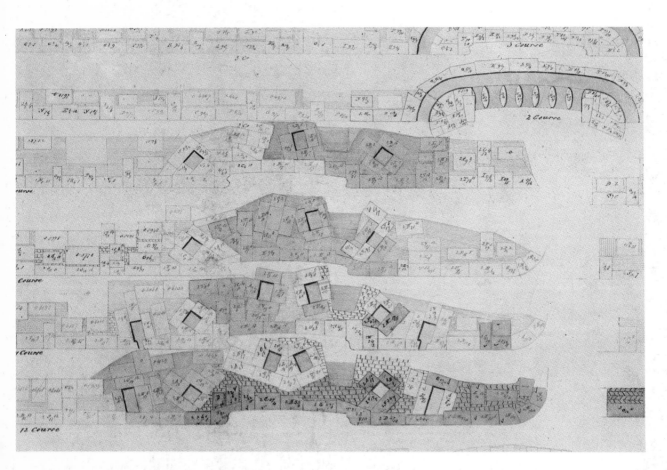

28 & 29 Designers sometimes lose control of projects of monumental scale; that Hartley never did is demonstrated by the fine detail on this window in the Dock Master's Office and the equally competent handling of colossal blocks of ashlar in the river wall, both at Salisbury Dock.

30 & 31 Masonry of the highest standard in Clarence Graving Dock.

HARTLEY THE STONEMASON

32 Hartley's incomparable masonry, a sort of functional sculpture, in the Clarence Graving Dock wall.

33 The roadway over the Leeds and Liverpool Canal. The stonework is magnificent.

HARTLEY THE STONEMASON

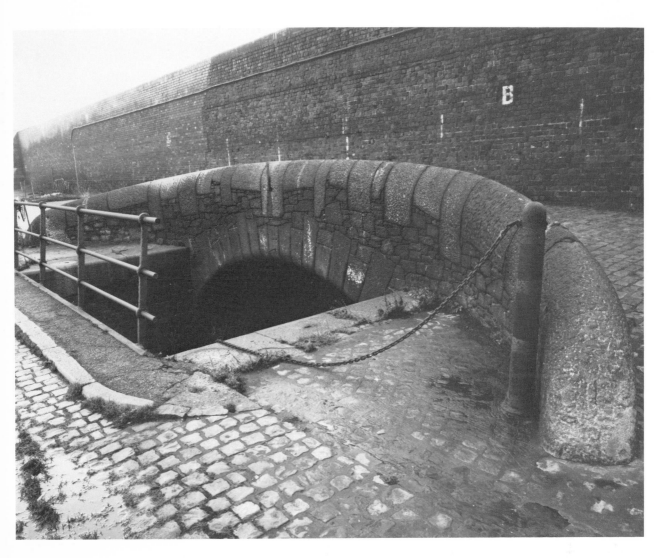

34 *Oak*, the coaster built for the Dock Surveyor's Department in 1836 to carry granite from the quarry at Kirkmabreck to the Liverpool dock works.

35 Hartley supported the construction of links between the docks and the canals which would facilitate the movement of materials and goods between the seaport and the inland manufacturing districts, all of which were served by canals. This 1930's photograph shows pottery crates being unloaded in Liverpool from the barge *Heatherdale* on the Leeds and Liverpool Canal. Such cargo was carried from the Potteries in narrow boats and transshipped at Anderton where it was transferred to barges on the Weaver Navigation. It was then carried across the Mersey and, via the docks, on to the Leeds and Liverpool Canal. Much of the pottery destined for export from Liverpool was stored in warehouses along the Canal until it was transferred to ocean-going vessels. Other important exports through Liverpool were cotton goods and machinery; major imports included sugar, wool, cotton and grain.

Canals and railways

36 Sections of a lock on the branch of the Leeds and Liverpool Canal as designed by James Thompson and agreed by Jesse Hartley in July, 1846.

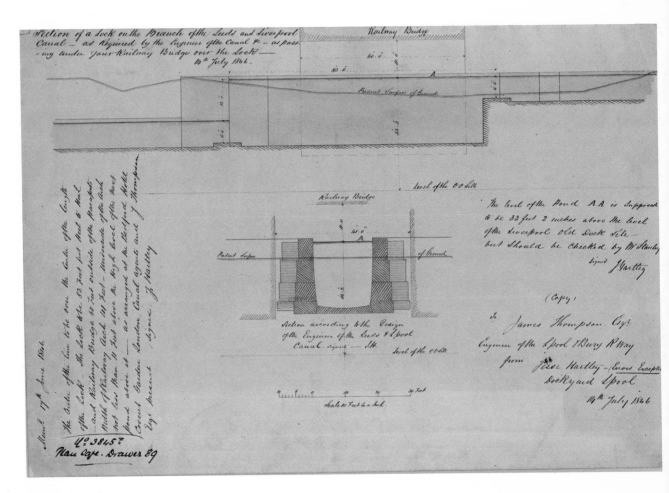

37 Distinctive Hartley masonry identifies this lock as one which he helped to design.

CANALS AND RAILWAYS

38 Plan and section of lock sent to Hartley for comment in October, 1846. The Dock Trustees bought the land and constructed a cut with four locks; the new cut was vested in the Leeds and Liverpool Canal Company who contributed £50,000 towards the cost of construction. The land between Great Howard Street and Regent Road subsequently was developed as Stanley Dock, and when the Salisbury, Collingwood, Stanley, Nelson and Bramley-Moore Docks were opened they formed a complete system which joined the Leeds and Liverpool Canal.

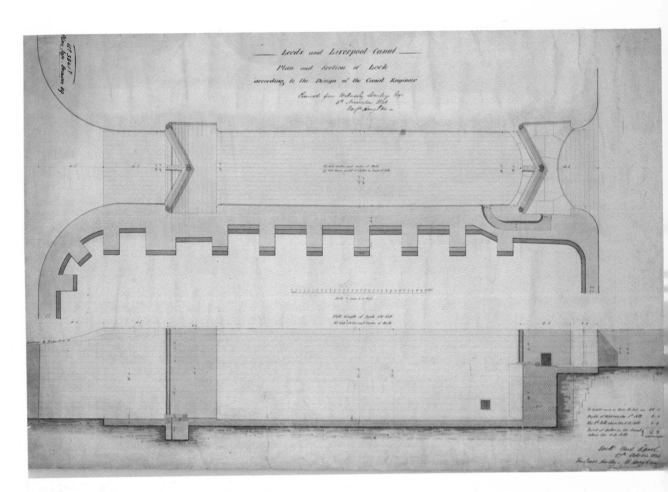

39 From its inception, the Liverpool and Manchester Railway was planned to extend through a tunnel under Liverpool from Edge Hill to Wapping, near the Queen's Dock. Branch lines and goods stations for other lines were soon built (Liverpool and Bury Railway at Lightbody Street, London and North Western Railway at Waterloo Dock, and Midland Railway at Sandon) and in 1850 Jesse Hartley prepared a plan for a complete dock railway system, one of the first in the world. The drawing below is Hartley's plan for the railway bridge over the east quay of Collingwood Dock.

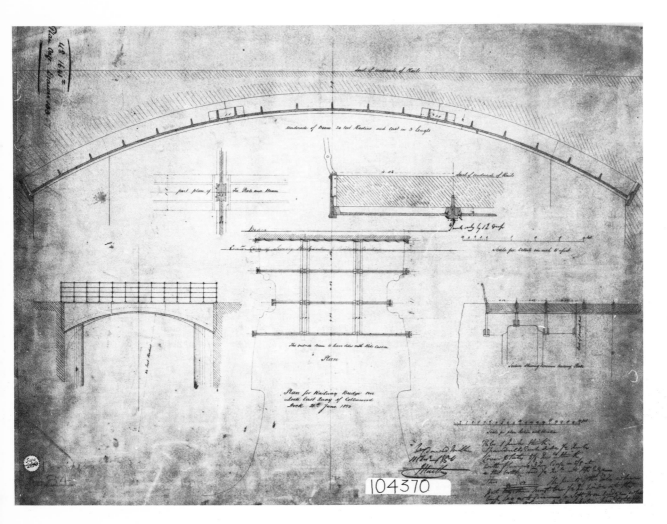

104370

40 & 41 The high level coal railway, at Bramley-Moore Dock, opened 1857. The development of rail links with the Orrell and Wigan coalfields during the 1830's and 1840's, and the increased demand for coal made improved quayside coal handling facilities desirable. These were provided by the construction of a high level railway connected by a viaduct to the Lancashire and Yorkshire Railway; coal was unloaded by hydraulic cranes direct from the high level railway to the holds of ships.

42 The dock railway system, initiated by Jesse Hartley, in operation during the construction of Gladstone Dock in 1925. Hartley, too, used the dock railway for this purpose and thus angered merchants who were unable to use it entirely for the carriage of goods.

Other projects

43 Marine side lever engine ordered in 1826 from Boulton & Watt, Birmingham for use in the Liverpool docks. Writing in 1841 to the Boulton & Watt Co. to ask for an estimate for a 15 hp engine, Hartley states that he has approached four Liverpool firms and Boulton & Watt. 'I fear you will not like to enter into competition – and that if you do, you will be too high – however time is the object – and the shorter the time before the delivery etc. the better chance the estimate will have.' (*Birmingham Public Libraries, Boulton & Watt Collection*).

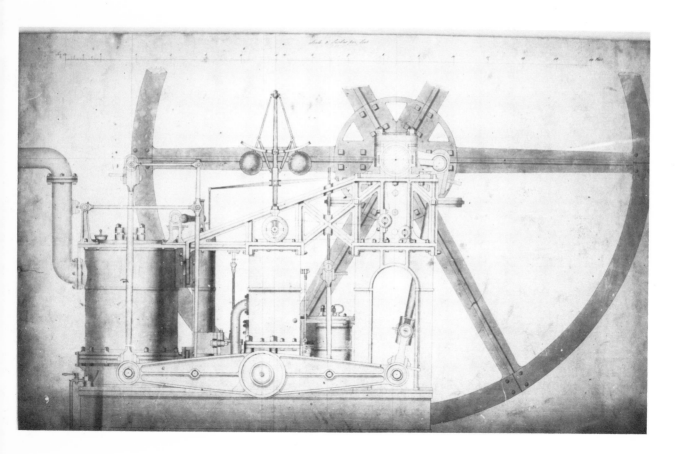

44 Beam engine and boiler designed in 1835 by Jesse Hartley. This steam engine is typical of those used to work machinery such as mortar mills and tilt hammers around the docks.

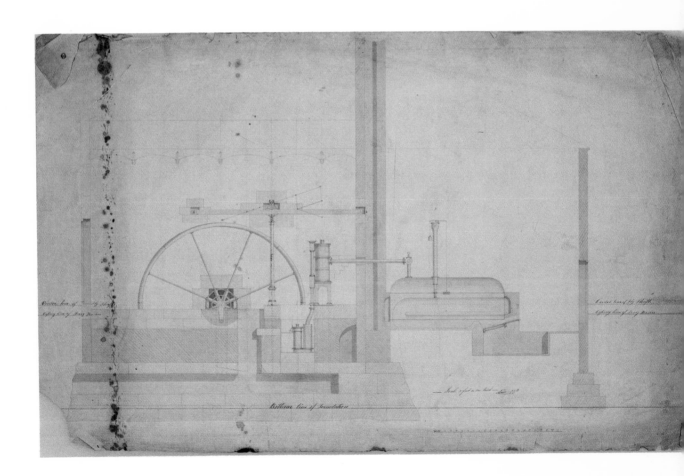

45 Mortar mill designed by Hartley. The huge scale of dock construction made on-site plant and equipment essential.

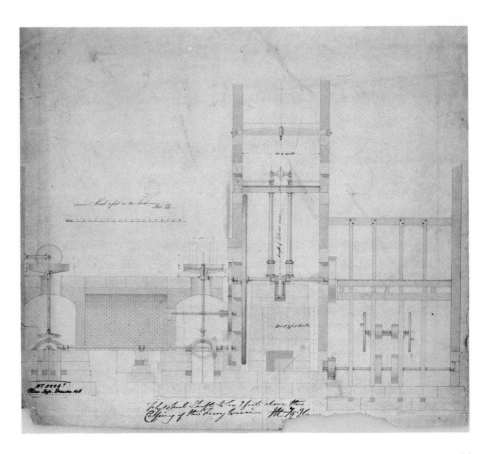

46 An 1835 design by Hartley for a variable-stroke pump for the Liverpool docks. Pumping was usually undertaken in conjunction with dock construction and with graving dock operation.

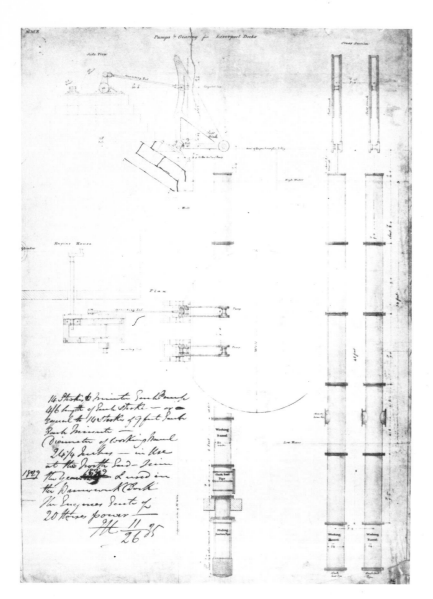

48 Sir W.G. Armstrong & Co's design for the hydraulic goods
lifts in the Albert Dock warehouses.

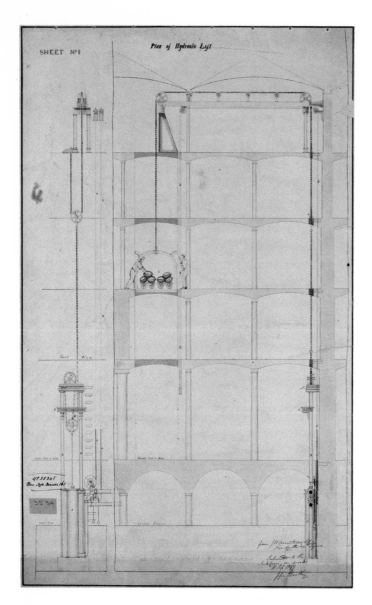

49 Following public exhibitions of an electric arc lamp in Liverpool early in 1852, the Dock Committee resolved in November of that year to erect a tower at the south end of Princes Parade 'for exhibiting the electric light'. This may have been the world's first permanent installation of an electric light for navigation.

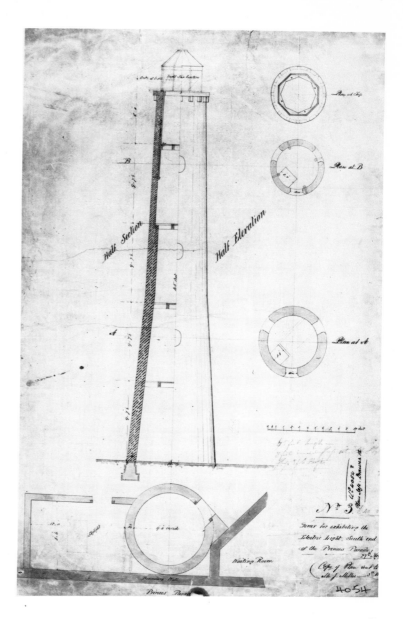

50 Hartley's secondary activities as architect, bridgemaster, canal and railway engineer sometimes obscure his larger role as civil engineer in charge of dock construction. But he was always conscious of his responsibility for development of the docks as a whole, and he produced a continuous supply of plans for new projects.

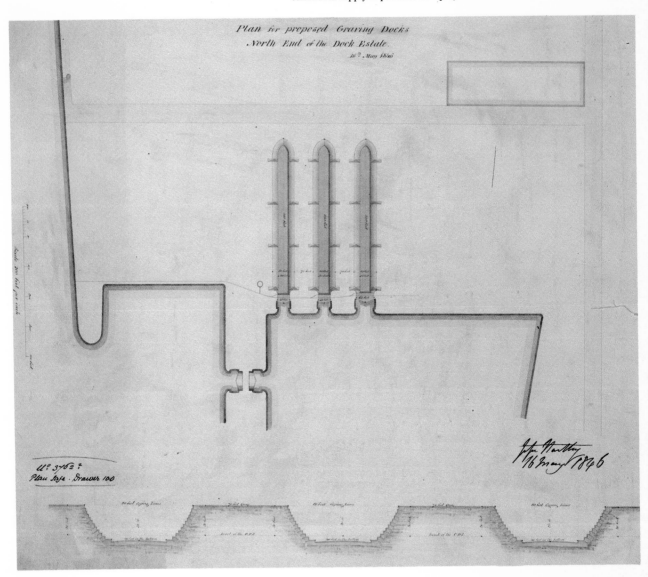